Do Not Feed The Bears

Overcoming:
Depression, Resentment and Anger

Dr. Cecilia Jackson

Dr. Cecilia Jackson

Do Not Feed The Bears
Overcoming Depression, Resentment and Anger

ISBN # 978-0-9620377-9-5
Copyright © in 2014 by Cecilia Jackson.
First Edition 2004, Second Edition 2012, Third Edition 2014,
Fourth Edition 2019
Printed in the United States of America
("I AM" Productions Publication)

Scripture quotations are from the King James Translation Bible.

Do Not Feed The Bears
Overcoming; Depression, Resentment and Anger

Table of Contents

Dr. Cecilia Jackson

Introduction

There are areas in every Christian's life that present challenges. These areas are usually the places where we are weakest. Of course, the desire of the adversary is to cause us to get weaker and weaker even to the point of allowing our challenges to overtake us. God has already shown in His Word ways we can become victorious over every challenge.

Some of the areas Christians often seem challenged in are: coping with depression, resentment, and anger. This reading shares simple Biblical help with what I have chosen to call "Bears". The allegorical thought of these challenge areas being "bears" we face, comes from my family's many visits to the mountains where one often reads literature about the hazards of feeding the bears and helpful pointers for camping outdoors; moreover, warnings from the rare times when we have seen, close enough, real "bears"! It is not a bright idea to feed these large lurking, hungry creatures. To do so will cause you and your loved ones to be hurt, and it could be fatal. So it is with the "bears" of depression, resentment and anger. This book shares in a brief, yet powerful manner, how to walk in victory over these challenges.

Included are strategies to overcome disappointments, sadness, suicide, self-pity, and other partner emotions associated with depression, resentment, and anger.

The work is great for small group bible study, large group teaching, and individual self-help study. It is anchored in truths applicable to both mature and adolescent audiences who may be facing these challenges as developing believers.

Dr. Cecilia Jackson

CHAPTER ONE
Depression – A Sunken Place

Have you sometimes felt you were so despondent that you did not want to get up in the morning? Have you been in a mental state wherein you could only cry, cry, and keep crying? Do you often withdraw from others, feel sorry for yourself, feel suicidal, extremely angry, eat and eat yet the hunger is not satisfied? Do you go periods of time without eating and you are predisposed with thinking about failures and disappointments? Do you experience restlessness and irritability? Do you sometimes feel guilty, hopeless or worthless? Are you often fatigue and feel loss of energy? Do you entertain thoughts of suicide or death? Are you experiencing loss of pleasure and interest in activities? What's wrong with you? You are depressed.

Depression is severe despondency, unhappiness, sadness, and gloom. It is typically felt over a period of time and is accompanied by feelings of hopelessness and inadequacy. Depression is considered a mood disorder presenting itself in down-trodden behaviors. It is more than just a bout of the blues; depression isn't just a weakness. Medical professionals consider it an illness.

The Bible describes depression as being in a sunken place where your spirit is sad. You are extremely discouraged which has caused a reduction in the quality of the life God has intended you to have. Not only is your vitality low, but your very will to fight can be challenged.

There are many things that can cause one to land in the condition of depression. Doctors have published recent study showing the medical and biological effects of light on human beings. Thus, Seasonal Affective Disorder (SAD) is said to be depressive episodes based on seasonal variations as connected to light or lack of sunlight or light. Certain people are sensitive in the winter where there is less exposure to sunlight. The cooler weather and shortened sunny days can have a negative impact on these individuals' mental health. Giving them excessive artificial light is supposed to help lift them from their "sunken place".

If you feel you have SAD, below are some lifestyle methods that can be used to cope with Seasonal Affective Disorder:

1)   Make plans to engage with others, socially.

2)   Regular exercise will release endorphins into your body and enforce positive feelings and increase energy.

3)   Eat healthy foods, including plenty of vegetables.

4)   Plan a trip; vacations in sunny climates can be uplifting.

5)   Open your blinds and curtains; be a friend to natural sunlight and the sun's rays.

6)   It's fine to consider a professional therapist for strategies.

7)   Schedule time for yourself regularly; develop a hobby.

People with negative thinking patterns and low self-esteem are more likely to develop clinical depression. Also a family history of clinical depression increases the risks for developing depression. Of course, difficult life events including: financial problems, marital problems, divorce, stress related to rearing children, little or no employment, changes in socio-economic status, and problems with family members in general are leading causes of depression.

Menopause, with its accompanying hormonal imbalances can cause depression is some women. Often restoring the proper hormones to nature's balance will relieve or eliminate depression in such cases. Physical problems can cause depression, such as surgery; or even the news of physical problems, especially challenging or chronic disorders, can cause one to sink to a low place in their emotions. This kind of depression is motivated by fear, the fear of mortal limitations and death. There are also other common experiences such as: loss of a loved one, feelings of non-accomplishment of goals or dreams, and the list goes on and on. All of these experiences are painful, especially when they can linger for months and even years. These experiences lead to a sunken place, a recessed feeling and moods of depression.

Depression, a sunken place, is one of the most common "mental" illnesses and it affects more than 16 million Americans annually (more women than men) according to the National Alliance on Mental Illness (NAMI, 2019). Depression knows no age, race or ethnic group. Neither does it have respect for gender, religion, employment nor health status. Unfortunately, many people do not believe depression is a serious illness until it has invaded their personal space and negatively affected loved ones, careers, overall health, and every part of their life.

Depression is one of the bears we as Christians often face. Yet, even though its presence is not wanted and often it comes upon us by surprise, we cannot waddle in the circumstances and let it keep us pressed down in a sunken place. To do so is like feeding a ferocious bear and the end result is it will come into your very home (your heart, your life) and destroy you. It won't stop there. It will affect the people you love most and will soon find itself comfortable in your home and the church.

Bears don't just choose to attack adults. Children are not a restricted area for them! If you do not choose to fight them off with the proper tools that will send them running from you, they will hang around until they not only destroy you, but your children, wife, husband, and friends too are all fair game. When you are depressed, your mental and emotional state has an impact on others.

Strategies for overcoming:

1)   Think, meditate, focus your mind on things that are good, pure, lovely and wholesome for your life. Avoid negative thinking and negative involvement (Philippians 4:8).

2)   Remember that the Lord will be with you. He will never leave you no matter what you go through, so do not be afraid, not be discouraged (Deuteronomy 31::8).

3)   When you pray and ask the Lord for help even though you are walking through depression, he will hear you and set you free from your trouble (Psalms 34:17).

4)   The Lord will lift you from any pit that you may fall into and he will set your feet upon a sturdy place once again (Psalms 40:1-3).

5)   Talk to the Lord about your personal issues, the things you know that have caused you to fall into a low, sunken place and he will shield you from further pain and will help to lift up your head to a high place because he loves you. (Psalms 3:3).

6)   Allow this condition to produce the power to persevere in you. Do not give up. Do not stay in that low place. Fight for your joy and happiness (James 1:3).

7) Do not allow others to make you feel disappointed about the choices you make. God will help you even though you may make unwise choices. He still approves of you and will help you climb back up to a place of success. Obey him by being glad, eating the food of joy (Ecclesiastes 9:7).

8) Pray for joy and peace concerning the things that trouble you and trust the Lord to help you in this situation and give you hope. Hope in your God.
He has the power and will help you out of this state (Romans 15:13).

Although the bear of depression may be a difficult challenge Christians face, we must above all, remember that God's Word says he has made a way of escape for us that we may stand in the midst of the difficulties. There is a way of escape! There is a winning posture we can assume for any challenge that we are faced with. The Holy Spirit has given us power to rise from any sunken place to an elevated place of victory!

Dr. Cecilia Jackson

CHAPTER TWO
Expectations And A New Attitude

Psychotherapists and other medical doctors have researched and come up with medications and helps for depression. A few common ones are listed: (antidepressants) Selective Serotonin Reuptake Inhibitors (SSRIs) – Prozac, Celexa, and Zoloft; Norepinephrine Reuptake Inhibitors – Cymbalta and Effexor; Monoamine Oxidase Inhibitors, and tricyclics. Psychotherapy for treating depression is as follows: Interpersonal therapy, and Cognitive-behavioral therapy, talking, music, drama, movement and art. Electroconvulsive therapy is also used when there is little or no success with antidepressants and psychotherapy. Although these methods have been helpful for some patients, rather than expounding on any of them, I choose to offer some Biblically based effective ways to overcome the sunken place of depression.

I have found that one of the most effective ways to move from a state of depression is to develop a new attitude about the circumstances you are faced with and to set reasonable expectations or goals for your life. Too many unrealistic goals can cause depression.

Short-term and long-term goals must be set for one's life. If all you have are goals that will take a long time to accomplish, you won't have any short victories to celebrate. You won't even realize that you are making progress toward those long-term goals because you won't be able to see the final results until later on down the road of life. Therefore, you can get depressed even though progress is being made when you focus only on the long-term results. Set short-term goals so that you can see God doing wonders for you on a daily and weekly basis. Celebrate those accomplishments! This will set you on a new course of having a new attitude about your life, one of success. There must be the attitude that God is good and that he is working all things out in your life for your good. Your attitude shapes your outcome!

Romans 8:28 "And we know that all things work together for good to them that love God, to them who are the called according to his purpose".

Many people set unrealistic expectations and become depressed and angry with God when their expectations aren't supported. Set realistic expectations. If you know it took you five years to gain an excess of seventy pounds over weight, don't expect it to take five days to lose the weight. If you were born with brown eyes, you will more than likely have brown eyes until Jesus returns. Don't pray for blue eyes and get disappointed when your eye color does not change. Buy you some blue contact lenses and be happy. If it takes four years of college to qualify for the kind of job you want, stop "claiming" the job position you don't qualify for, believing you will have it given to you. Go to the business office of the college of your choice and fill out financial support applications and scholarship applications to get the money to attend college to qualify for the "dream" job you want God to give you. Next, go to school and study. Then graduate from school and go get the job. Chart your time frame for this long -term goal and celebrate God meeting your needs in other positions of employment, short-term, until your final desire comes to pass.

Be realistic. If the father of your children is not financially supporting his children and you are financially depleted trying to care for them, pray for God to change his heart and save him and walk by faith to believe his heart will change; however, in the mean time until the prayer is answered, go to the legal authorities and process whatever paper work that needs to be processed legally in order to get the support that is due you to help care for your children! God is not getting any glory in your children suffering and you smiling on the outside, while frustrated, depressed, and torn up on the inside because your "X" is taking good care of his new lady and her children, yet neglecting his responsibility for your children. Get out of that sunken place and set some realistic expectations and God will meet you in the midst of your plans!

Whatever the desires of your heart are, set both short and long-term goals and move strategically towards accomplishing them. This will provide the fresh roses of experiencing daily, weekly, monthly, and annual successes as you proceed to the completion of seeing your long-term dreams fulfilled. Remember, God is in the plan with you. He had you in mind even before you were in your mother's womb.

Jeremiah 29:11 "For I know the thoughts that I think toward you, saith the LORD, thoughts of peace, and not of evil, to give you an expected end".

Ecclesiastes 3:1 "There is a time for everything, and a season for every activity under the heavens"

Job 42:2 "I know that you can do all things; no purpose of yours can be thwarted".

John 10:10 "The thief's purpose is to steal and kill and destroy. My purpose is to give you a rich and satisfying life."

Dr. Cecilia Jackson

CHAPTER THREE
Think Optimistically

I am convinced that circumstances are sometimes not as bad as they seem once we deal with the reality of reasonable expectations and developing a new attitude about out situations. However, even when things are genuinely difficult, we must learn how to cultivate habits of positive thinking. This is merely thinking in a manner that scripture dictates. Paul told the saints at the church in Philippi to think on the things that were true, lovely, just, and pure.

Philippians 4:8 "Finally, brethren, whatsoever things are true, whatsoever things are honest, whatsoever things are just, whatsoever things are pure, whatsoever things are lovely, whatsoever things are of good report; if there be any virtue, and if there be any praise, think on these things".

He said that if anything was worthy of praise or to brag about, anything worthy of giving time to in one's thoughts, then it should be those things that are good. That is still the word of God to us today. Don't give time to thinking about sadness or pain; it will only keep you depressed, prolong your feelings of anger, and become a harbor for resentment. That's feeding bears.

So, what does one do while going through difficult circumstances? Even in the middle of the experience, find something to be thankful for. Be positive. Look for and point out something good, something you can be glad about even before the end of the hard time. Positive reflection contributes to a changed attitude. Often we are not capable of changing out heart, but a mind (thinking) change can lead to a heart change if we continually ask the Holy Spirit to do the work of transformation in us. We can keep growing, evolving, and improving while experiencing what could potentially cut off all life in us. The Spirit of The Lord will change our heart when we obey the Word of God and condition our minds to think His way while walking in faith during our challenging times. We are not thanking God for the mess, but thanking him while enduring and developing as we change, become strengthened, and more mature in the lifestyle of Christ. We are not to thank the Lord for our condition, but to thank Him IN our condition, trusting Him that HE will bring us out.

1 Thessalonians 5:18 "In everything give thanks: for this is the will of God in Christ Jesus concerning you".

Paul and Silas exercised the secret of being thankful and thinking optimistically in all things. When they were thrown in prison in Philippi, beaten and put into stocks, at midnight they started to sing praises to God. Even the other prisoners began to listen to their new songs created while experiencing extreme circumstances (Acts 16: 11 – 40). The end result was good. They were eventually set free from prison. This was the result of their optimistic attitude while they were going through something awful. These were ordinary men, no different from you or me. What could happen if you started to sing and praise God through what you are going through! God would set you free from it.

Psalms 28:7 "The Lord is my strength and my shield; my heart trusts in Him, and I am helped; therefore my heart exults, and my song I shall thank Him".

Psalms 106:12 "Then they believed His words; they sang His praise".

Hebrews 13:15 "Through Him then, let us continually offer up a sacrifice of praise to God that is the fruit of lips that give thanks to His name".

Psalms 104:33 "I will sing to the Lord as long as I live, I will sing praise to my God while I have my being.

I went through an illness one summer that really set me back, so I thought. It was during a time that I was working on the completion of my Masters of Education degree at Xavier University. The ministry was growing and moving and I was right in the middle of some very exciting things when a physical attack came upon me which restricted me to being home, and the inability to move my body to even go to the restroom without my husband's assistance. I had never felt pain in such magnitudes. The greatest pain was when we took the children to the train station to meet my oldest son as he was coming home that summer from college and I would have greeted him in a wheelchair. Persons, who know me, know that I am not one to be immobile. The physicians had diagnosed me with inflammation of the brain and symptoms of a mild stroke. When I heard these words I felt myself sinking to a low place, depressed, discouraged and feeling my faith was challenged in the area of believing I would be healed. I cried each time my husband had to help me from the sofa to the restroom. I had taken enough medicines to lose track of how often I was taking this pill or that, yet nothing seemed to give me relief unless I was in such a deep sleep that I felt in a state between consciousness and unconsciousness.

I did not have the strength to sing aloud, but I began to sing softly to myself and to sing to my spirit new songs of praise to God and prayers for God's supernatural touch. It was time to be optimistic. I had already told my husband not to tell the details of my condition neither to the saints nor to some of my family members. It was not a matter of pride, but an issue of not wanting to alarm others and not wanting anyone feeling sorry for me. It was an assignment for me to go through the process of my own test as I learned to trust God and move to another dimension of faith. Also, I did not want to begin feeling sorry for myself. I stopped taking most of the pain medication and began listening to the audible word of God. I prayed, and praised and worshipped my heart into a positive attitude, an optimistic posture, a joyful outlook, and a mindset of hope. My proclamation was, "I will live and not die, in order to declare the works of the Lord, which is my purpose (Bible, Psalms 118:17)". I will NOT die, but I will live and proclaim what the Lord has done for me! I found a way to be thankful while enduring the pain, and experiencing the depression; consequently, this determined action caused me to see and feel myself walk into deliverance, freedom from a down-casted spirit. I declared that God had His own way of allowing me time with Him to get to know Him better. I declared it to be a season of rest for me, no matter what medical science and medical terminology called it. I went on a journey with the Lord that led me to total healing. Because I went through the process, the result was when I greeted my son, he saw me standing, not confined to a wheel chair! When I returned to the house of the Lord, I returned with strength and joy! Part of what I had to do was, think myself happy, believe against what appeared to be fact and stand on what was fact; by his stripes I am healed!

Isaiah 53:5 "But he was wounded for our transgressions, he was bruised for our iniquities: the chastisement of our peace was upon him; and with his stripes we are healed".

I was in graduate school when the attack came, so God moved on the hearts of men and gave me favor! The university accepted my doctor's reports and worked with me to do independent studies in order to graduate on time! My job awarded me the sick time needed to start work two months later than scheduled for that Fall Semester! All was well. I learned from Paul and Silas to determine the atmosphere in what "seemed" to be my prison, so that freedom would come and my prison became my pedestal to rise!

An optimistic view in the center of what may seem to be an eye of a storm causes us to think, act, and react according to scripture. We rehearse the words of Paul when he said, "We are afflicted in many ways, but we are not crushed. Sometimes we are puzzled, but we are not driven to despair. We are persecuted, but not forsaken. Sometimes we are struck down, but we are not destroyed. We always have memory of the death of Jesus so that the life of Jesus will be made visible in our bodies (2 Corinthians 4:8-10)". We are alive and create life when we think optimistically!

2 Corinthians "4:8-10 We are troubled on every side, yet not distressed; we are perplexed, but not in despair; Persecuted, but not forsaken; cast down, but not destroyed; Always bearing about in the body the dying of the Lord Jesus, that the life also of Jesus might be made manifest in our body".

Dr. Cecilia Jackson

CHAPTER FOUR
Don't Feed The Bears Of Resentment And Hurt

Your honest emotional responses to the following questions and statements will help you to determine if you are harboring resentment in your heart.

1) Have you lost your job and there are others whom you feel should have been downsized rather than you, and this disturbs you?

2) Do you feel upset because you never seem to have the money for the things you need, but it bothers you that others who seem not as righteous as you, are prospering, experiencing financial security?

3) Does it make you angry to see others dreams come true while your life's plans seem to stand still?

4) Did a religious leader disappoint you and you'd prefer to never be around them, or other believers and churches as well?

5) Do you always seem to be at the right place at the wrong time in order to get the opportunities you feel you deserve, while others seem to walk right into doors of opportunity?

6) Does your health, ethnic designation, education status, or appearance seem to prevent you from getting a break in life?

7) Did your children, wife, husband, friend hurt you and cause you to avoid establishing relationships with others?

8) Do you frequently use these words, "I won't forget that", "I can't forgive you for that"?

9) Do you "fake" happiness by smiling around friends and associates to cover your true, hidden feelings of unhappiness?

10) Do you speak in a sarcastic or demeaning manner to or about a person(s)?

11) Are there people whom you feel were unnecessarily hurtful, thoughtless, or mean to you for no reason, therefore you are not comfortable around them and you rehearse their maltreatment of you?

12) Do you feel the people closest to you have not done enough for you or have no compassion for you?

After responding to these questions, think about the meaning of the word "resentment": to hold a grudge against someone, to be annoyed with individuals because of an insult or disagreement, to hold deep-seated ill will against another person, to be unable to release ill feelings about another person. Resentment is the mental process of continually replaying a negative feeling and the negative events leading up to the negative feeling that caused the bitterness to lodge in ones heart. The individual is affected emotionally, spiritually, and psychologically by the memory of the incident. When he or she is disappointed and hurt and allows the hurt to germinate in the heart, the root of resentment (which is also called bitterness) becomes lodged in the heart. Resentment is characterized by a critical attitude and unforgiving spirit. One's thoughts and actions are colored with a deep hurt that eventually produces a spiritual death and pain that impacts everyone the offended person is around.

After this personal inventory and looking at the definition of 'resentment', you should now know for certain if you are carrying resentment. If you have answered "yes" to several of the listed questions, you are harboring bitterness and resentment.

If you are not feeding the bear of resentment, skip this chapter and read on. If you are feeding this hungry creature that wants to live in your heart, then read this chapter prayerfully and allow the Spirit of the Living God to touch your heart and change you. If your answer was yes to any of the survey questions – you should read this chapter.

Resentment is most powerful when it is felt toward someone whom the individual is intimate with because it leaves the individual feeling betrayed as well as resentful. The state of the person is emotionally debilitating resulting in anger, edginess, hostility, cynicism, sarcasm, all of which are barriers to healthy relationships and positive personal and emotional growth.

Resentment is a basic choice to refuse to forgive. It is the rehashing of ones painful past. Often the offences are "perceived" offenses because the individual has not been able to abandon personal issues in their own distant past. The root problem is usually the result of backed –up unhappiness and harbored venom from those years past. Any present incident is simply a trigger valve that releases what was already resident in an individual.

Perhaps childhood, parental, friendship, neighbor, school, spousal, and/or personal feelings of failure or betrayal and feelings of neglect are some of the real root causes for resentment.

Consider the fact that holding to grudges and hurts paralyze an individual from moving on with his or her life. You become a slave to the resentment when often times the person you resent has moved on and may not be aware of your resentment. You nullify your prayers, your faith, your happiness, your pleasure, your rest and sleep, and even your peace: like being a driver who is constantly being followed no matter which highway he takes, which driveway he enters, or which lot he tries to hid his car in. Living with resentment is like taking a poisonous drink expecting another person to get ill, when all the time you are consuming poison that will kill you.

Holding on to grudges and resentment takes a concentrated effort. One has to utilize a large amount of energy to nurse a grudge, and to remember why they are so angry and upset, especially after time passes. Individuals who have resentment also attempt to persuade others and to justify the magnitude of their ill will and anger. They rekindle the flame of passion for the grudge if it begins to wane. If they continue to carry the offense long enough, it will damage them and others in their circle of relationships, even their relationship with God. Nothing anyone has ever done to you can be worth a broken relationship with God. Let it go and allow the refreshing waters of the Holy Spirit to heal you. You owe this to your own self; help and healing is the Lord's best for you and is available to you.

For some reason, nursing a grudge can feel good at first, especially if someone has really wronged you. What happens is the feeling of self-pity is cultivated. For example one starts to think:

1) After all, life isn't fair!

2) One thinks too many opportunities have passed them by.

3) They have strong adverse feelings because they are not as financially secure as their neighbors.

4) They feel their friends and people they trusted most, have hurt them.

5) They believe they've had more than their share of bad circumstances. So, what develops with this way of thinking is a seed of hurt begins to grow into a full-sized bush or tree of resentment. What must be realized is people can hurt themselves when they hold on to grievances, pains, resentments, jealousies and the like.

Esau hated Jacob because of the blessing which his father had blessed him with and he felt the decision was unfair and deceitful. Esau said to himself that the days were coming close when his father would soon die and go to paradise. He thought in his heart to kill his brother Jacob. The mother, Rebekah, heard about Esau's plans and told Jacob to get out of town quickly. These brothers missed years of relationship. The Bible narrative tells of how they finally were reconciled many years later and they wept and rejoiced (Gen. 27). We learn from this story that resentment hurts us and others in relationship around us. Without a doubt, Rebekah was affected by the broken relationship of her sons Esau and Jacob. Follow the Bible narrative to see how Rebekah and the family handled this harbored resentment.

How can we prevent the "bears" of resentment and hurt from hanging around our cabin and coming inside to dwell? First, I'd like to suggest that you minimize your disappointment in others by recognizing that no one is perfect. You are not perfect. It is inevitable that people will hurt you. Some will hurt you intentionally and set out to cause trouble for you. Others will not mean you any harm, but their actions or lack of response will hurt you.   Whenever you are involved with others, you set yourself up for hurt and disappointment. Yet, at the same time, you set yourself up for happiness, simply because people are human. That is just the way it works with human beings. So realize that no one is perfect and love them for how God has made them in spite of their weaknesses and the way they sometimes behave. Minimize your disappointment in the behavior of others by remembering that no one is perfect, not even you. Consider that if the individual is a believer who is determined to develop into a mature Christian, then God is still working on him or her, and he is still working on you.

Jesus knew mankind would error when working together, simply because of human nature. Some say love your neighbors and hate your enemy, but God's command is to love your enemies and pray for those who do you harm so that we can all develop as sons of our heavenly Father. He causes the sun to rise on the evil and the good and sends rain on both the good and the bad. He says if you love only those who love you, the reward is small because that is easy to do and even the non-believers can successfully practice that law. So, if we practice this behavior then we as Christians are no better than non-believers and our minds have not been renewed by the word of God. We are to observe the higher practice which is to love those who do wrong to us.

Matthew 5:10-12 "Blessed are they which are persecuted for righteousness' sake: for theirs is the kingdom of heaven. Blessed are ye, when men shall revile you, and persecute you, and shall say all manner of evil against you falsely, for my sake. Rejoice, and be exceeding glad: for great is your reward in heaven: for so persecuted they the prophets which were before you".

We can learn to love people for who they are only if we look to God for our reward. We cannot depend on others and their approval. We are free from the bondage of human expectation as we look to God for his love and approval. Grudges are released if we first do not allow them an opportunity to lodge in our heart. Second, if we expect others to error and remember they are not perfect beings, then we will not become so disappointed when others make mistakes and hence hold resentment against them as associated with their errors. This frees us from taking on the bear of resentment.

Furthermore, we can avoid feeding resentment and hurt by allowing the healing waters of forgiveness to flow through us even when others do not. This is a personal choice. Grudges can be eliminated if we keep hurt from becoming full-blown by quickly forgiving the person who has hurt us. I really mean, quickly forgiving the person. We must be immediate with our forgiveness, whether we are the offended party or the one who offended someone else. Sincerely apologize and make restitution immediately. This enables you to move on and not become bitter. It keeps the heavens open to your prayers and causes your praise to be heard by God and your relationship with the Lord pure.

The apostle Peter called Jesus his closest friend. He walked and talked with the Lord for three years. He understood the mission of Christ clearly, possibly more than others as we consider some of his responsibilities in scripture. In spite of this, Peter denied his Lord three times, not once or twice. He repeated his weakness. Jesus responded by asking Peter to make a recommitment of his love. Then he allowed Peter to repent and begin again with no soiled past (John 21). This is a fine example of forgiveness and a decision to not allow resentment to rule because Peter's denials could have cost Jesus his very life.

We find another reliable example in Paul. God gave him another opportunity after failure. Paul had been a murderer and a zealot, yet God extended to him a new life. This was contrary to the feelings of the leaders in the early church. They were not eager to give (Paul) Saul a second opportunity because they were afraid of him since his past actions were brutal demonstrations towards Christians. Barnabas received Saul and was willing to give him the benefit of the doubt. Barnabas was willing to risk his life for Saul, believing he had truly changed. That kind of action established the way, and set an example for Christians today.

The young nephew of Paul, John Mark, wanted the excitement of going on a missionary journey, but soon after he left Paul and Barnabas, for some reason John Mark decided that he did not want to continue, so he left and went back to Jerusalem (Acts 13). Later, when Paul wanted to return to the churches they had previously ministered to in order to check up on the believers there, Barnabas suggested they include John Mark, but Paul disagreed. He was reluctant to involve the young man again, because of the previous experience of him leaving the ministry before the mission was complete. They decided to separate into two groups: Barnabas took John Mark and sailed to Cyprus and Paul and Silas went to Syria and Cilicia (Acts 15). Later in Paul's ministry, he mentions John Mark as being a very useful servant (II Timothy 4:11). We need more Barnabas-like spirits today – those who will extend to others a second chance. We also need more people with the spirit of Paul. He was willing to forgive and forget John Mark's past and his weaknesses and activated his forgiveness by spreading a good reputation about his brother Mark going forward with Barnabas in ministry; when he could have spread destructive information at the time of separation.

Reflect on these situations relative to today's Christians. Believers seem eager to tear one another down at times, rather than build one another up in Christ. This has frequently happened at times of separation regarding different views about how to implement ministry. Individuals have been called "cursed", sheep thieves, and other degrading names. In some extreme cases leaders have forbidden their members from associating with other members of the body of Christ completely. Such actions are certainly motivated by the "accuser" of the body (satan) and not motivated by the love and leading of Christ. Such experiences in the Christian walk can leave bitterness and resentment if a believer is not mature enough to walk away with love and forgiveness in his or her heart.

My husband and I had a similar experience wherein we had the opportunity to make the choice of forgiving and not harboring resentment; or not forgiving and walking away with anger and bitterness in our hearts. This was a situation wherein we had labored many years in faithful support of a ministry, and extended communication and letters of support and love to the pastor and leadership team when the time came for us to relocate and to continue to fulfill our purpose in God. Because our previous relationship had been wonderful, we made every possible effort to go forward with vision and had every expectation that good relationships would continue. We were shocked and hurt when we later learned the pastors had circulated harmful, degrading, inflammatory literature to other ministries throughout the city and to dear friends, misrepresenting our intentions. The materials circulated were not only untrue concerning ministry intents; but they were an attack on our personal character, which had taken years of consistent living to build. Of course this was not a pleasurable feeling, especially when these persons were those whom we had placed ultimate confidence in, had built long term relationships with, and had served and protected in ministry with all our heart for many, many years. We had considered them our spiritual fathers, so the hurt was deep and painful.

What does one do? Make mature and liberating choices. Realize all human beings are subject to error. Choose to forgive the parties involved, refuse to hold resentment in your heart, and leave it to the Lord to take care of the rest. Also, walk in close relationship with other strong believers and leaders who can support you in receiving your healing, rather than cuddling the hurt and making it your friend.

31

Dr. Cecilia Jackson

You may say, "That is not an easy thing to do". I tell you from experience this was not an easy thing to do, but it became easier and easier as we were determined we would obey God's prescription for healing and walk forward in peace, joy, and the spirit of forgiveness. We all learn and grow through the things we suffer. It is a part of the process of the call. In addition, we learn in the fire or crucible of events what our own character is made of. My husband and I received many calls from others who knew us well, and had worked with us for years in ministry, and even in that ministry. They were appalled at the situation. We refused to entertain even that intended (positive) communication as support; but instead, asked them to pray for all involved because "Godly sorrow works repentance to salvation (Bible, 2 Corinthians 7:10)".

Others we worked with in the secular field heard about the matter and were incensed and encouraged us to take legal action agreeing to help with financial support to do so. We had paperwork and written documentation that could have supported this idea and won the case, but we had to ask ourselves who would win in the end. We could have walked away with finances from legal action for being slandered, but that would not have appeased the hurt from the destructive arrow of Christian brothers. Only the Holy Spirit could have really won in this case and that was if we allowed him to get in, and stay in the arena in the center of the crucible -- and that is what we chose to do!

Ephesians "4:31-32 Let all bitterness, and wrath, and anger, and clamour, and evil speaking, be put away from you, with all malice: And be ye kind one to another, tenderhearted, forgiving one another, even as God for Christ's sake hath forgiven you".

We surrounded ourselves with believers who not only interceded for us, but also encouraged our little ones who, of course, were affected by the situation. We were determined to be better and not bitter from the matter, and God met us in the middle of the mess! He made a mess into a miracle!

On occasions we were at services and prophets called us out and described how, the enemy had used people we loved to throw fiery darts at us and a stone that would have destroyed us, but the angels of the Lord stood between the destroyer and us and delivered us. One prophet prophesied that the arrows were sent to pierce, but He/God had reversed them and was using them to point the way to greener pastures where he had already ordained for us new relationships on the foundation of God's love and His Word. Our hearts rejoiced, especially since God had sent the word of prophecy to us from vessels of whom we had never met nor even seen in our lives! We needed those words of love, direction, and support from God to assure us that we could walk through that storm and that the word we had been taught was indeed true, even though the teachers chose not to walk by that word. Because of our obedience, not only did the Lord bless, heal, keep, and revive us – but he used this trial for our "good" and launched us forward into new fruitful revelations and relationships! Above that, he blessed and anointed our seed!

Why did God move for us? Because we took the first step and moved toward God by choosing to follow scripture patterns while experiencing the pain of the trial. We refused to feed the bears of resentment and hurt and chose to walk in forgiveness.

Matthew 6:14-15 "For if ye forgive men their trespasses, your heavenly Father will also forgive you: But if ye forgive not men their trespasses, neither will your Father forgive your trespasses".

The Bible states that if we forgive men, our heavenly father will forgive us, but if we do not forgive our brothers and sisters neither will God the father forgive and remember us. We refused to nurse the pain, but allowed the Lord to heal it. We refused to shut off those who acted ungodly, but chose to forgive them. These were still our brothers and sisters in the Lord. We still visit the congregation today when we choose too!

Hebrews 12:14-15 "Follow peace with all men, and holiness, without which no man shall see the Lord: Looking diligently lest any man fail of the grace of God; lest any root of bitterness springing up trouble you, and thereby many be defiled".

God is using this experience to also minister hope and life to others who are going through hurts from Christians in the Church. Just as God had those who were as Barnabas to us, we are now as Barnabas to others. If you choose to be better and not bitter, God will use your life to bless others. It will be a testimony of the power of God that is able to heal, deliver, forgive, and teach you the love and compassion of God.

A final way to keep resentment and hurt from building up is to minimize our own disappointment with God. Follow me on this one. It seems a strange bit of advice, but it's important. Often we set ourselves up for disappointment in God because we tell God how to answer our prayers and how to run our lives. We give him great details; we become presumptuous in our expectations of his honoring our requests, often not consulting him for his plan for any of the episodes of our life. Then, when our prayers are not answered the way we thought best, or the way we told Him to answer, then we feel God has failed us or let us down. Our faith begins to weaken, we wonder if God really cares, and the seeds of resentment against God are sown and begin to grow in our heart.

Remember the prayer in Matthew chapter 6 requests the kingdom of God to come and His will to be done on earth as it is done in heaven. Although it is scriptural to pray for the desires of our hearts to be met, what about praying for the will of God for our lives more often than praying for our desires? I have found that this works to minimize disappointment and makes us more receptive to what God is doing and wants to do in our lives. By praying this way, we pray for the will of God to be done in our lives first and that he orders our steps so that our will lines up with His will. In his will there is no disappointment because it is the path that pleases him, thus it launches an arrow of peace and joy that goes straight to the heart giving us freedom from hurts and resentment.   There is no peace comparable to resting in the bosom of His purpose, His destiny for your life. Resentment and hurt are bears we cannot afford to befriend.

Dr. Cecilia Jackson

CHAPTER FIVE
Anger Is A Bear

Anger is a feeling of antagonism and displeasure usually resulting from opposition, conflict, or the inability to manage a specific situation and incapability of having control over personal life. It is severe despondency and dejection typically felt over a period of time and is accompanied by feelings of powerlessness or failure to handle relationships with others on a consistent and positive basis. It is actually a mood disorder presenting itself in either a defeated posture or a posture of superficial power and control. It's not just intense hype. Incendiary anger isn't just a weakness; it is considered an illness linked with associative behaviors such as: holding grudges, being remorseful, reacting cynically, being spiteful, holding resentment, getting revenge, and often volunteering threatening outbursts displaying lack of bodily control.

In deviant crimes, anger has its roots in resentment and usually "long term" resentment that has arisen from feelings of frustration and anxiety caused by a lack of feeling personal control. Often the resentment turns to anger even as early as childhood and continues into adulthood. Sometimes individuals attempt to cope with their anger through fantasy, but when they realize it is mere fantasy, the anger returns. This is because the root of bitterness has not been addressed. Eventually these individuals actually move into violent action and the anger is severely displaced. It targets the individual's children, spouse, friend(s), neighbors, members of the religious community and even persons he or she does not know. Persons can be seriously hurt and even killed because of displaced anger.

An example, is a father who comes home from work and instead of confronting the person on the job who caused the anger, he verbally or physically attacks his spouse or his children, masking the root of his anger.

37

Another example is perhaps an unmarried mother who is frustrated because of stress on her job, so she comes home yelling, screaming, and verbally and physically attacking her children. Anger is often an action of impulse and violent outbursts, which could lead to fatal consequences. The sad conclusion is in most cases the individuals blame the victims for causing their violence.

Anger and Violence
Anger is a root of violence that is attached to an overwhelming event and can throw a normally functioning person into emotional and physical pain and suffering that can lead to violence. This cycle can be seen in not only adults, but in children and teens. Unresolved anger keeps adults and children trapped in a hopeless cycle of self-destruction. Anger is active in: corporate circles, hospital settings, violent-prone communities, homes (domestic violence and child abuse), television programs that impact adults and children, subways and streets, educational institutions from elementary to middle to high school and college, even in churches.

Note the following:

- Studies show that in general, people with higher exposure to anger, anxiety and duress are more than 1.3 times prone to death from cardiac arrest and coronary events. Anger affects an individual's physical health Anger can actually kill you by triggering deadly heart rhythms (Reuters Study, Chicago).

- There is an increase in violent crime resulting from anger (gang related crime, domestic violence – a parent killing the partner then the child, hate crimes (race and gender related), and crimes of retaliation related to road rage and random "hand" signals of anger and hate.

• There is an increase in crime and death (suicide) related to anger in schools due to: bullying, gender diversity issues, even academic performance and acts of anger related to non-relenting determination to disrespect authority; which studies show that such oppositional defiance of adults is directly related to anger and resentment associated with family and community issues.

• The increase in juvenile crime is astounding! Crimes are no longer committed primarily by individuals ages 18 and older. Statistics indicate an immense increase in anger related crime committed by children and teens ages 13 -17 (https://www.aacap.org).

• There has been a notable increase in aggressive violence and anger depicted prominently in public media such as: video games, archaic games, adult cartoons, movies, reality shows, and even talk radio that reflect a global community whose constituents have been adversely impacted and exposed to more deviant, hostile behavior.

• More and more media attention and social media information is being published revealing hostile verbal dialogue and in some cases physical altercations (clergy to clergy, clergy to member, member to member) about positions and offices, decision making, doctrine, property settlements, deviously dysfunctional families, gender choices, and domestic violence in the church. Both subtle and shrewd behaviors of anger are surfacing in these areas of Christian relationships leading to what the Bible calls sin.

Positive Anger
Surely the destructive energy of the "bear" of anger is at work in our society; however, anger is both a positive and negative emotion that can serve as a function for protection or for destruction. We all experience anger at one time or another in our lives, but it does not mean that we experience this emotion in the same way. It can vary from a mild intensity to an extreme explosion and each one of us has a different level of control over these feelings.

When anger is positive it allows us to be assertive, but with control. For example if someone feels they are taken advantage of in a situation, they may be capable of being assertive with control; whereas another may be assertive but unable to maintain control.

There is a difference between anger and hate. Anger is a sign that we are alive and well whereas hate is a sign that one is sick and needs to be healed. Healthy anger can drive us to do something to adjust situations in our lives that may need to be changed. It can energize us to make things better. We are allowed to be angry, but when angry we must not sin. Anger can be a positive force or a negative energy.

Ephesians 4:26-27 "Be ye angry, and sin not: let not the sun go down upon your wrath: Neither give place to the devil".

What are some ways to relieve ourselves of the negative energy of anger?

Forgiveness and Memory
One way to relieve oneself of anger is to simply admit you're angry. Identify your emotion and take steps to be healed from it. Ignoring your feelings won't make them go away so don't brush them off as just an insignificant emotion or reaction. These same actions will continually surface in situations in your

life until you face them as bears and allow the Word of God and the Spirit of God to help you win the victory over vicious cycles of allowing them to dominate your personality and your life.

1 John 1:9 "If we confess our sins, he is faithful and just to forgive us our sins, and to cleanse us from all unrighteousness".

One way to rid ourselves of the negative energy of anger is to simply forgive. In other words you can get angry with a matter, but immediately work on forgiving the person for whatever was done to make you angry, even the things that happened in your past and distant past. Sometimes when our mind says we have forgiven a person who wronged us, we feel we have not forgiven because our emotions still remember the anger of that time. This is the battle God wants to give us understanding and victory over. Often people are still angry and are still holding resentment and bitterness against a person who has wronged them, while that person has forgotten he has ever done anything wrong. Who does this harm? Surely not the person who was guilty of inflicting the hurt upon the individual, but the victim who was hurt and chose to hold on to the pain which festered into anger. It is a strong "bear" but it can be brought to its knees when the victim learns to forgive.

Matthew 6:15 "But if ye forgive not men their trespasses, neither will your Father forgive your trespasses".

Matthew 6:25-26 "And when ye stand praying, forgive, if ye have ought against any: that your Father also which is in heaven may forgive you your trespasses. But if ye do not forgive, neither will your Father which is in heaven forgive your trespasses".

Memory is part of our brain function. It is a God-given ability. Some things are stored in the short-term memory and others are stored in the long-term memory. The time length of memory usually depends upon how often something is rehearsed. That something can be a math lesson, a memory scripture, or an offense. That's why it is important to avoid rehearsing hurt and anger and any negative occurrences, because it will become a part of the long-term memory and thus harder to forget. This increases the risk of a person becoming bitter and holding resentment. When one is quick to forgive, the pain, or offense lies only in the short-term memory; thus the incident is more quickly forgotten. Yet, because the mind can remember the offense, does not mean it hasn't been forgiven. It takes time to forget, but forgiveness can happen quickly. Our intricate web of memories is not like a slate that we can just wipe clean. So, although we can remember an incident, we could very well have already begun the process of consciously forgiving the person associated with the experience.

Forgiveness offers us a way to minimize the pain associated with the ill done and the opportunity to go on with our life. As we go on with life, time will cause the memory to fade away. We can see persons who have wronged us in a new light of compassion not necessarily justifying their acts toward us, but releasing both them and us from the negative situation and negative energy of anger. This moves us toward total healing and reconciliation.

When we start to understand forgiveness the way scripture requires us to live, then passages in the scripture become clearer to us. Ephesians chapter 4 tells us to not let the sun go down while we are angry. This lets us know that conflict may not be solved before the sun goes down; however, we are to forgive quickly – before the sun goes down (before we go to bed). We are not to lie down at the end of any day with anger in our heart. We can operate the process of forgiveness each day. We are to practice forgiving, even as God forgave us, then we can exert every effort possible to work with the person to completely resolve the conflict. One must understand however, that endless discussion on some issues will not ever bring them to resolve. In such cases when you have done all you can do, move forward in peace with your brother. In other words, agree to disagree and move on in love.

Peter asked Jesus how often he should forgive a fellow Christian for sinning against him. Jesus answered him saying he should forgive seventy times seven.

Matthew 18:21-22 "Then came Peter to him, and said, Lord, how oft shall my brother sin against me, and I forgive him? till seven times? Jesus saith unto him, I say not unto thee, Until seven times: but, Until seventy times seven".

In other words we are supposed to be willing to continually forgive one another. Obviously after forgiving someone repeatedly, we won't immediately forget what happened in succession after each incident. However, God begins to remove the pain of the encounter and as we allow God to continue to work in our lives the spirit of forgiveness, we are made free. In time, as we refuse to dwell on the hurt, the angering experiences will become less memorable. Persons who continually entertain conversations about hurting incidents will slow this process of forgiveness and healing. Rather, continue to cast that concern, weight and care upon the Lord.

Being Still
One of the most difficult things to do when we are angry is to BE STILL. It is even harder to make an immediate decision to repay good for the evil done. Both seem to be unnatural response! Yet, that is exactly what Paul tells the church at Rome to do. He says to bless those who persecute you and do not curse them. He says to rejoice with those who rejoice and to cry with those who cry. Furthermore, he instructs the saints to live in harmony with one another avoiding haughtiness, by being lowly and never conceited. Paul instructs the church again, to repay good for evil and to live peacefully with everyone. He instructs the believers to avoid seeking vengeance because he

says vengeance is the Lord's responsibility and it is certain that He will do His job and repay. In the latter part of Romans chapter 12, God tells Paul to tell the church to feed their enemy if they are hungry and to give them water if they are thirsty; finally he says to overcome evil with good (Romans 12). These behaviors enable believers to avoid feeding the bear, anger. One can be sure that if anger is fed, a lot of other old and young bears who are friends with anger will begin to hang around your home, your heart. A few friends of anger are: hatred, resentment, bitterness, sickness, and murder. Instead of yielding to these behaviors, BE STILL and wait, and think instead of acting too hastily. Society today encourages us to defend ourselves, fight back, and be aggressive. There are certainly times when we do need to be more aggressive or forward, but in the heat of anger, being cautious in the wise way of response instead of fanning the flame of fury which causes more heartache. Practice BEING STILL, taking time to cool off.

Be careful. Do not allow anger to force you to be out-of-control. The Word of God gives some examples of persons who allowed their anger to get out of control. When Cain and Abel brought their offerings of the fruit of the ground, Cain was very angry and his countenance fell (he became saddened and full of rage). The Lord asked him why he was so angry and why his countenance had fallen. He warned Cain that if he acted properly he would be accepted, but if he chose to lose control and remain angry, then sin was waiting at the door or his heart with the plan to control him. God wanted Cain to master sin and his own anger (Genesis 4). The end of the story reveals that Cain failed the test. He was so out of control that he eventually took Abel out to the field and killed him. Thus, the result of his anger and loss of control was the death of his brother. Believers in our day are still killing brothers and sisters in the Lord because they are not able to control their emotions, anger, and hot temper! Don't be one who causes death: death of dreams, literal death, emotional death in family relationships, psychological and spiritual death in relationships in the body of Christ, because of the bear of anger.

Saul could not master his anger and it caused him to throw a spear to try to kill David. His uncontrollable anger forced David to run for his life (1 Samuel 18).

Some of us may have experienced times in our lives when we allowed our anger to get out of control resulting in embarrassing ourselves, wounding others, and ruining our good Christian witness. Although anger can be a natural response, how we respond to the energy of anger becomes a choice and an act of our will. We can choose to respond with the mind and character of Christ, or to respond in the strength of our own will. Positive results come when we allow the Holy Spirit to control our will and by doing so, we control our anger, which is His will.

Strategies
How do we avoid feeding the bear of anger? How can we direct the energy of anger toward good? How can we develop control over our anger? Simply obey, practice God's word:

1) Be angry, but do not sin, only commune with your hearts at night and learn to be quiet, be still (Psalms 4).

2) Give a soft answer; it will turn anger in another direction (Proverbs 15).

3) Be quick to hear others, speak less frequently and learn to listen (James 1).

4) Don't get angry so fast because anger does not reflect God's righteousness, and will result in the loss of control and even death.

5) Do not have communication or conversation with bitterness, malice, murder, and slander; but be kind, tenderhearted, and forgiving to others just as Christ forgives us (Ephesians 4).

6) Quickly forgive, even before the sun goes down and in time with the help of the Holy Spirit, you will forget.

7) Use the energy of anger to help you develop creative ways to build relationships and avoid behaviors that will entrap you in anger.

8) Allow the peace and love of God to prevail in your actions, responses and decisions.

9) Let God's peace become part of your lifestyle, avoiding anger. Anger will cause discord and this contention and fighting spirit will cause you to error. "An angry man stirreth up strife, and a furious man aboundeth in transgression (Bible, Proverbs 29:22).

10) Do not have close association and friendship with individuals who cannot control anger. You are likely to develop the same habits in your life and will not have the accountability necessary to help you improve the challenges in your life. Close relationship with an angry person will cause you to become ensnared in the trap of anger rather than delivered to a place of peace. "Make no friendship with an angry man; and with a furious man thou shalt not go: Lest thou learn his ways, and get a snare to thy soul (Bible, Proverbs 22:25).

These strategies above project the beauty of overcoming a fault, the spirit of anger, by doing it God's way. Instead of carrying around a heavy load of anger, you can experience the joy, peace, and victory of allowing the Father to take the weight of anger from you and release you into serenity and calm. This will bless you and all those in your relationship circle.

How do we avoid feeding the bear of anger? How can we direct the energy of anger toward good? How can we develop control over our anger? Simply change your lifestyle and commit to obeying and practicing God's Word.

Dr. Cecilia Jackson

CHAPTER SIX
Exhortation

At times in all of our lives we have fallen short, or given up the victory to an area of weakness. It is important that we persevere to perfect Godly character in us. We must not feed the bears (areas of weakness) in our lives, but feed our strengths and feed on His word. The bears of depression, resentment, and anger come to tempt all of us at some time in our Christian walk, but God has given us power and authority that we may triumph victoriously over them! I exhort you to use the reliable instructions given in this text as practical tools of great power for choosing and fostering an authoritative and overcoming life. The content and scriptures in this text will strengthen and equip you to *Overcome Depression, Resentment, and Anger. Do Not Feed the Bears!*

Dr. Cecilia Jackson

References

Basic Concepts of Depression. Eugene S. Paykel, Dialogues of
        Clinical Neuroscience, 2008 September; 10(3):279-289.
Forgiveness and Resentment. Midwest Studies in Philosophy.
Getting Back to Happy. Marc & Angel Chernoff, 2018.
Handling Anger. Livestrong.com Archived from original on
        January 23, 2011.
How to Get Rid of Resentment and Emotional Abuse.
        Psychology Today (2013).
Http://www.livestrong.com/article
Major Depressive Disorder Among Adults. National Institute
        of Mental Health..
National Institute of Mental Health: "The Numbers Count:
        Mental Illness in America, (Science of our Mind Fact
        Sheet Series. Accessed August 20 Retrieved, August,
        2014.
Overcoming Emotions that Destroy: Practical Help for Those
        Angry Feelings that Ruin Relationships. Chip Ingram,
        January 2013.
Retrieved, August, 2014. 9http://www.livestrong.com/article.
The Holy Bible (King James, Amplified, Message, New
        America Standard).
The Things We Keep. Sally Hepworth, 2018.
Understanding Emotions. Oxford: Wiley-Blackwell. P.88 – 90
        ISBN 978-1-4051-3103-2.
Uprooting Anger: Biblical Help for a Common Problem:
        Robert D. Jones, 2019.
What Causes Depression. Harvard Health Publications.

Books Published By The Authors
Drs. Michael & Cecilia Jackson

1.   **9 Gifts of the Holy Spirit** - The Scriptures confirm that God operates through a person as a co-operative act; man does not become a puppet, or act unconsciously, or go into a trance. Rather, he must co-operate with the Lord to express what God wants to say in the way God wants it expressed. The Holy Spirit can manifest any one of these 9 gifts through any believer anytime that He will want to do so. Each one of these gifts are major gifts in that they are all direct, supernatural, miraculous manifestations direct from the Holy Spirit Himself and any Christian can and should keep themselves in proper place and perspective to operate any of these 9 gifts.

2.   **(A Synopsis) Differentiating Religion, Tradition, Church, & Kingdom** - This work is a "synopsis", of four topics: Religion, Tradition, Church and Kingdom. We are communicating foundational Biblically based material and research on these topics with the prayer and expectation that the Spirit of wisdom and revelation in the knowledge of the Son of God will rest upon anyone who reads this text so that a solid, general understanding will be embraced concerning the believer's inheritance in Christ through His church (Ephesians 1:16-23). Furthermore, we pray and expect that you will be motivated to continue further study and consideration of the power resident in the believer through understanding and differentiating Religion, Tradition, Church and Kingdom.

3.   **Touching A Woman's Heart** - This text is dedicated to Biblical answers in response to real issues that concern women of today. The author presents analogies, allegories, and anecdotal episodes that parallel conditions of the natural heart and cures, to conditions of the spiritual and emotional heart of women and cures. Biblical scriptures and solutions are offered. The focus and strength of this work is the

presentation of Biblical solutions to paralleling spiritual and emotion conditions that concern the heart of women.

4.   **Be Made Whole** - The contents of this book reflect the healing of God for the whole person as revealed through study of the woman in Matthew, chapter 9.

5.   **Belonging** - Belonging is a simple systematic Bible teaching for new converts becoming new members of a local church. It teaches basic Biblical government, sacraments, and foundational necessities for growing up in Christ. Books may be ordered specifically for your church to assist you with grounding souls for the Kingdom.

6.   **Bold Truth** - This text is to encourage parents to become more familiar and comfortable with basic information on sexuality, so that they become the channels to route information to their children. The purpose of this content is also to educate young people on facts concerning sex, birth control, and sexually transmitted diseases. Truth takes the mask off of the lie, and exposes knowledge that silences curiosity, which is a chief energy in youth that causes many young believers to fall captive to the devices of Satan.

7.   **Maintaining An "OPEN WINDOW" Of Heaven** – A comprehensive review of the spiritual principles of how we break the poverty curse through tithing, and to maintain an open the window of heaven from God.

8.   **Get Her Back on Her Feet** - In scripture, we are often likened to Sheep who are cared for by the Good Shepherd (pastors) or the Great Shepherd (The Lord). So, we understand that The Lord cares for us and loves us so much that we boast in the benefits of belonging to Him and being surrounded by His care. We also as believers have a responsibility to show demonstrative love to one another.

9.   **Categorizing Spiritual Gifts** - It is said that it through these "lenses" (gifts) that we SEE the world or our approach or focus in life. To sum things up each believer has at least one definite Motivational Gift, at least one Gifts of the Spirit and may grow into a Five-Fold ministry to Christ's Body – we must discover "who" we are!

10.   **Dialogue Between the Watchmen and The King** - "A thorough and clear explanation of the relationship between the watchmen (intercessors) and the king (leader). This is a necessary teaching for leaders and those who minister in the role of the watchmen - indispensable lessons tools on practices in prayer for all believers."

11.   **Discern Deploy The Heir Force** – God is the pre-eminent one, over all – both angelic and demonic powers and He has delegated much authority over to us. While many ministries are called to teaching, preaching, and demonstrating in the area of Deliverance, this work focuses on teaching, preaching and activating in the area of God's angelic force. It is important to know the role angels play in the lives of believers and to understand what the Scriptures teach regarding these powerful beings. One of the most awesome benefits God has given His believers and His church is angelic help. It is necessary information for victorious Christian living.

12.   **Dominion For Practical Singles** - We believe that in this latter part of the 20th century and in the early years of the 20th century God wants a breaking forth to occur within the second-largest people-group in Christianity, the unmarried population. We hear the clear voice of the Lord in the land and His Word to the Church concerning the unmarried believers. There is a harvest coming that will be greater than the world has ever known. There is surely a Church within the Church that will move on with the spirit of the Lord. God is calling the unmarried population in his Church to rise, to be equipped to minister to the harvest that His

Hand will bring in, and to be a part of the Church within the Church that will move on to a higher dimension in Him.

13. **Do Not Feed The Bears** - Some of the areas Christians often seem challenged in are: coping with depression, resentment, and anger. This reading shares simple Biblical help with what I have chosen to call "Bears". The allegorical thought of these challenge areas being bears we are faced with, comes from my family's many visits to the mountains where one often reads literature about the hazards of feeding the bears and helpful pointers for camping outdoors; also, from the rare times when we have seen, close enough, real "bears"! It is not a bright idea to feed these large lurking, hungry creatures. To do so will cause you and your loved ones to be hurt, and it could be fatal. So it is with the "bears" of depression, resentment and anger. This book shares in a brief, yet powerful manner, how to walk in victory over these challenges.

14. **Do You Have The Right Attitude?** - No building stands without having, as its base, a solid foundation. Attitude is the "advance man" of our true selves. Its roots spread inward and upward, anchored in past experiences, and the fruit branch spans outward exposed for all to see. Yet, who controls this attitude? You do! You must always improve the attitude you possess within yourself. Learn to overcome fear and to deal with rejection and failure in order to increase your productivity while saving time and money. Your attitude is 100% completely within your control!

15. **Finding The RIGHT Woman** - This book is a guide for all those men (and women) who will represent His godly character and standards in their lives and surrender to solicit God's help in solving one of life's most important decisions – finding the RIGHT woman.

16. **From Press To Passion** - "God is moving us from a place of "press" to "passion" - the Lord is moving the body of Christ from a place of struggling, intensifying, and

accelerating laboriously as we move forward, to a place of moving forward with joy, passion, enthusiasm, ardor, devotion, affection, loyalty, and zeal!

17. **Go-Forward!** - We will always be tempted to turn around, give-up or quit but the Christian life is such that there is ONLY one Godly option ... and that is to Go Forward!

18. **Hannah** - Hannah is a book that teaches the importance of subduing the voice of the accuser – satan -- when he comes to rob you of dreams, goals, desires, and the hope of your future by stamping "barren" on your spiritual womb, helping you to give birth to areas that were once barren.

19. **It's A Wrap!** - Each believer in the Kingdom of God has been saved from hell's fire by the blood of Jesus Christ and is given a purpose, a calling that should be the path of his or her journey as daily life is lived on earth. Relax from your fears of not accomplishing what God has purposed you to do. Your future is safeguarded, defended and fortified even by the Lord and his angelic hosts! This is a truth that is without controversy. When you believe this in your heart and allow the Lord to settle it deep within your human spirit, the Holy Spirit will be at liberty to release the miraculous in your life and the marvelous in your daily path now and as you walk into your God ordained future. Your destiny is secure!

20. **Kingdom Quest I** - A Fundamental Trio Teaching Series on Victorious Kingdom Living: DO NOT FEED THE BEARS (Victory Over Depression, Resentment, and Anger), IT'S IN THE HEM OF HIS GARMENT (How to Be Made Whole), and FROM PRESS TO PASSION (Adjusting Your View of Kingdom Advancement).

21. **Rebuilding the Economy of the Global Kingdom of God** - So Nehemiah's approach was from a business perspective and also a political perspective, but it was for the purpose of the Kingdom of God. A vision must be crafted and embraced by believers globally who have a mind to see

economic re-construction in every area of society: religious, social, political, economic and otherwise. When systems are aligned with God's Word, a great shift takes place and we, the church and the Kingdom of God move to a position of economic security, strength and health rather than insecurity, weakness and frailty. This is one of the greatest times in the history of the world, an era or epoch of time in which the Lord wants to unify his people around a plan etched out and supported by his Grace and Anointing; a God-established pattern for re-building our global economy in the Kingdom. This text gives an expository pattern from the Biblical approach of Nehemiah who embraced the opportunity to re-build the economy of Jerusalem.

22. **Releasing The Leader Within** - God is raising up disciples who will be developed extensively in their character and their hearts. "No longer will He accept leaders who He's gifted but having NONE of HIS Grace within them "embarrass" the Church!

23. **Remembering Her: The Power of a God Inspired Mother** - My mother, Alma Ingram-Jarmon-Davis; was an exceptional, incomparable, amazing mother. Her love for my siblings and me knew no boundaries. This simple, powerful work is dedicated to men and women globally who might see glimpses of their mother in the life of Jochebed who made a way out of no way.

24. **Principles of the Kingdom** - Many people have heard the term "Kingdom of God," but few really understand what it is. Throughout the entire Bible, this was the central message! John the Baptist preached the Kingdom of God, Jesus preached it, and the apostles preached it. The last question that Jesus was asked before He left the earth was, "Lord, will you at this time restore again the kingdom to Israel?" The coming Kingdom of God is the message that God wants to convey to every person on earth. The crucial question is, will you be a part of it? We define some of the Kingdom Principles spoken of through the Bible to define the Kingdom of God.

25. **God's Woman of Excellence For Today: The Shunammite Woman of II Kings** - This book is simply sharing what the Lord impressed in my spirit regarding areas that women of God can build up, in order to become WOMEN OF DESTINY, WOMEN OF EXCELLENCE, in our time. Actually it was birthed from a message the Lord gave me in preparation of a ministry engagement. During my time of study, I was encouraged to improve my attitude toward serving, and motivated to take the challenge of becoming a woman of excellence. This book is for women and men who desire to understand this subject through the life of a great woman in scripture, whose name is not recorded -- The Shunammite Woman.

26. **Scribes: Write To Publish!** - If you see yourself as the creative director of your book(s) from concept to completion and beyond, then you can be a self-publisher. In this book, we will discuss briefly the history of writers, the types of publishing, the professional writing process, the levels of editing, journaling, book layout, cover design and printing, ebooks, marketing techniques and conclude with literary midwife services. This book will give you many insights into the progression and production of literary manuscripts.

27. **Simply Praise!!** - This is Praise Class 101 simplified – everything you ever wanted to know about praise but was afraid to ask!

28. **Step Back To Sprint Forward** - Basic starting techniques are vitally important in sprint races. When one is a successful runner, his success is because of his basic foot position on the starting blocks. The heel will be off the back block, with lots of pressure going through the back foot as a foundational position. Often runners STEP BACK and LOOK BACK in order to secure that they are in proper position to finish the race with winning status. Winning a race depends on how an athlete orchestrates his step backward and his looking back at this foundational position as preparation for going forward. The foundation affects

the smooth execution of the whole race. Parallel the technique of this natural race with that of the spiritual race we run in Christ. To finish the Christian race, we too must take the time to STEP BACK and LOOK BACK as foundation for moving forward. The only way we can grow and go forward is continuing to reflect on Biblical prototypes and foundation given by God to dictate a God inspired future.

29. **The Bible Mesmerizing, "In-Your-Face" Info** - Every narrative, proverb, historical account, song, battle, and any other presentation of material in the Bible, was written to both caution and encourage readers. Reading and studying Biblical truths also makes the believer stronger in the Christian faith. Furthermore; Biblical information is fascinating, mesmerizing, and in-your-face (confrontational). God had you in mind! It is material that challenges the reader in decision making, life stabilizing, life upgrading, and life changing principles.

30. **TRU - The Tongue of the Learned for Cultivating Racial Unity** - God's incomparable love wants everyone to be reconciled to him through his Son, Jesus Christ (John 3:16-17). This is the ultimate goal for the creator of the whole universe. Thus, the words we say and the things we do should reflect unity with the God of all creation. Racial disunity is often the thing that divides and pushes individuals far away from the desire to know the ONE true and living God. As Believers, Christ followers, it is the time and season to stand on the scriptures and principles of God concerning the use of words with wisdom in order to inspire generations and shift the negative conditions in our country and even in parts of the world. The goal is that men will be reconciled to God.

31. **Tithing Your Tithes** - The manifestations and blessings of tithing have eluded most Christians because they have lacked specific knowledge, or they did not have a clear image of tithing to begin with ... Change will not occur in you by being passive; you must be stead

fast in your heart - violently committed. God wants to move into your household and direct your path!

32. **A Tool Kit for Understanding Prophets and Prophetics in the Church** - In this generation, God is reinstating the gift and office of the prophet in his church, so questions relating to the definition, authority, function, mandate, credentials, and authentic call of the prophet are on the hearts and minds of many believers. Questions are being asked, not only for understanding how to support what is authentic, but how to disengage with what is anti-scriptural. This is not an all-inclusive Tool Box on the prophet and prohetics, but a SIMPLE took kit that rightly gets one started in the basic, Biblical apostolic foundation of the church prophet and the operation of prophetics in the church.

33. **Make Your Valley Full of Ditches** - The Lord will sometimes answer our prayers in a way that we do not expect, but when we obey His plan by faith (even if it defies our natural, usual, human way of thinking) the results will come forth, manifest, and make us glad! Tell a friend or neighbor to dig, which means to perform an act of faith and wait on God's promise to respond to his or her faith. Agree to dig a ditch as well, and make an agreement to support each other, as you trust God to fulfill his promise of your faith. God will move!

34. **Wailing Women Warriors Win** - A wailer is one whose purpose and desire is to wail until change comes, to wail until chains are broken, to wail until intervention comes that institutes change! When women who know the Lord begin to wail, change will come. God will divinely intervene and answer their cry.

35. **Who Is God?** - "Who Is God," is a comprehensive systematic bible study that leads individuals into relationship with Christ and establishing the foundation that is required in order to mature in Him.

36. **The Divine SPIRIT Of God** - There is a need for simple, Biblical teaching on the Holy Spirit in Kingdom based churches today. For many who are in and coming into church as new and recent converts, there exists misunderstandings in regard to the Spirit of God, His purpose, function, indwelling, and benefits for the believer and the church. This book is appropriate for all ages of believers and non-believers who desire simple yet accurate Biblical answers regarding The Divine Spirit of God.

37. **You Have A Gift** - Most Christians have heard of spiritual gifts, some believers know their spiritual gifts and have been developing them by regular use; yet, there are many believers who have not heard of spiritual gifts and are not sure if they understand them or what their spiritual gifts may be. If you don't know about spiritual gifts, you will void God's best plan for your personal life. One of the most exciting personal experiences of the Holy Spirit is discovering, understanding, and using your gift(s).

38. **From Dung To Dominion** - The Word of God includes many narratives that speak to us today when we take time to read and study them with our lives in mind. This book, From Dung to Dominion, is part of the story of the life of the Prophet Elijah. It summarizes how Jezebel, the Phoenician princess and queen of Israel, retaliated against Elijah after he had destroyed the altars of Baal and killed the false prophets. The book likens us to Elijah and shows parallels to possible excerpts from contemporary believers; including the feelings of defeat but moreover, the powerful victories and strategies for success from the chase of evil in the lives of believers.

39. **Help -My Child Doesn't Look Like Me** - Families established across national, racial, ethnic, and cultural boundaries represent a growing demographic in the United States (US) and are adding to the broadened diversity of family unit forms. In recent decades in the United States, it has become more common for American parents to blend into their homes children from other countries: Korea, Guatemala,

China, India, Africa, Russia, Nepal, Mexico, Latin and Central America, Vietnam, Asia and other countries. When one adopts internationally, he brings a child from his or her country and culture to a foreign country with its own unfamiliar culture. If the family's physical and corporal features are the same as the new child's, then adjustments may be relatively non-problematic. However, it is much more often that international adoptions comprise parents who bring into their families a child who looks entirely different than they do. Moreover, the cultural and ethnic differences carry their own set of challenges. The results, such families can face struggles both inside and outside of the home.

40. **The Hand of God** - As the Church continues the upward climb of dominance and preeminence from the abyss of the "Dark Ages" to its place of pre-determined glory through Jesus Christ, of ruling among the nations, God is manifesting His Plan, as the Holy Spirit releases revelation after revelation of what the Church is destined to be. One such example is the scripture of Ephesians: 4: 11-13. I have been asked on numerous occasion what is the "5 Fold Ministry? Many have heard of the term but really don't know what it means and they have never asked within their own church exactly what is the "5 Fold Ministry."

41. **An Etymological Teaching On Race, Culture, and Ethnicity (International Adoptive Parenting)** - The book An Etymological Teaching on Race, Culture, and Ethnicity (International Adoptive Parenting) is a tool that assists adoptive parents, prospective adoptive parents, and introductory professionals with pertinent definitions, instructions, and benefits of embracing multi-cultural, multi-ethnic, and multi-racial differences in adopted and pre-adoptive children.

42. **Eliminating The "Fear" Factor** - At some time in life, we all have experienced "fear" or anxiety of some kind. Not sure of how the body or the mind responds to fear nor the overall impact fear has on the physical and mental

faculties, it is likely that we have allowed fear to occupy too much space in our lives. This fundamental book is designed to open new doors of thought regarding how to manage or eliminate fear factors and move forward in new victory and authority.

43. **Roots of the Church (Depiction of Today's Ecclesia)** – A concise historical review and preview of the various styles of Churches from the children of Leah and Rachel.

44. **ERA of the ATYPICAL** - The Lord will use prolific and illustrative acts during this era to strengthen Kingdom of God advancement in the earth today. There is an aggressive return of the supernatural, the atypical. The creative and creation will SEE Christ through the manifestation of the sons of God. This IS the ERA of the Atypical.

45. **God's Recycling Plan For Your Life** - God has an instinctive (innate) RECYCLING system on alert in your body that recycles what is harmful to a state of normality, a state of healing and wholeness. This system parallels the natural cycle of seasons in the earth. So, no matter the seasonal cycle or trauma that humans in society experience, even during a pandemic, God's recycling system remains intact. His built-in healing functions of recycling never fail. I am astonished that when I get a scratch, a cut, a bruise, or any type of minor injury; something interesting happens in my body. It begins to heal itself. Cuts, scratches and bruises heal themselves without us telling them to do so. They just get on with the healing process spontaneously. Even if the bruise is as blue and black as a night's eclipse, it finds its way back to normal skin color eventually. Even a burn, will instinctively begin the process of blistering, drying, scabbing over and in due course, begin making new skin. God surely has a recycling plan.

46. Creation Groans for the Sons of God To Manifest- A believer who ministers (serves) what he or she does in love, peace, enthusiasm, and joy, while understanding God's purpose for him or her will move into a place where he or she is a candidate for the manifested glory and miracles God desires to release in the earth. The EARTH IS GROANING for us believers (creatures) to manifest the power of God now! This cannot happen if our life is one of pressing, laboring ahead, moving drudgingly along, painfully pushing forward, doing what we do in an agonizing manner, and feeling distressed and stressed about the work of the Lord and the responsibilities we have committed to do in the Kingdom of God. The Bible states that the very earth is waiting on you and me – the powerful sons and daughters of The Lord, to manifest His glory! A passion for Him, His presence, and His work are the only ways this level of manifestation of his dynamos power can happen in and on the earth!

47. Being A Water-Walker - Granted this author's story (Dr. Michael Jackson's) is exceptional; but he believes that ALL believer's stories are unique. Being a "WaterWalkers" is the typical new-covenant heavenly lifestyle of all true Holy Spirit filled disciples of Jesus. As you read this book just listen, surrender, and allow the Lord to redesign your life into something more than spectacular ... the challenge is to join me as we are transformed into WaterWalkers for Jesus!

48. The Ministry of the Apothecary: You, the Healing Perfumer - Through Jesus, as worshippers, we always bring the fragrance of God with us wherever we go. Aaron's sons did not understand what they were doing fully. They did not know that they were only a type of something far better to come. As we do the work of the apothecary and make sweet incense, we will see change come in every area of our lives, not because we plead but because we praise, not because we beg but because we bow, not because we are powerful, but because He is All Power. This work of the apothecary, the perfumer, the chemist, the holy pharmacist, IS the blending of stacte, onycha, galbanum, sweet cinnamon, sweet calamus, myrrh, cassia, olive oil, and frankincense -- the gums and spices broken from trees, beaten very fine and blended for oils for anointing and for the act of burning on the Incense Altar for sweet fragrance. The total picture speaks of the preciousness of Christ's mediations, wooing, invitation, and beaconing of our praise and prayer to be released before Him. Such expressions of adoration are sweet to God's nostrils. This ministry of the healer is the work of the New Covenant priesthood. We are the compounders, the druggist, the perfumers, the pharmacists of a new and better covenant who carry the responsibility of healing and wholeness for ourselves and others.

49. **Seeing BEYOND The Activity: Discerning The Spirits** - We must understand the authors' mind when they wrote book of Corinthians, then we'll have to call it what Apostle Paul calls it. Although we use terms very colloquially, in application, the discerning of spirits is exactly that; it is a gift given for the purpose of knowing the spirit behind activity and behaviors. Often believers label this gift in 1 Corinthians 12:8-10 as discernment. This is incorrect. Believers can discern various situations and circumstances through the divine leading of the Holy Spirit, but that is not the function of this particular gift. The gift of discerning of spirits is quite clear. It is the supernatural ability to look into the realm of the spirit and clearly see and know the spirit motivating a person or situation to perform or present in a specific and particular way. The operation of this gift is imperative for all believers and absolutely essential for prophetic people. As a prophetic person, you deal with uncommon realms of events and sometimes unusual opposition. The enemy will attempt to weaken your integrity with false spirits sending false messages through polluted people. This includes a wrong spirit concealing behind the scenes and motivating a person. Prophetic people must have the ability to SEE and KNOW the spirit behind the activity. That is the operation of this wonderful gift given to the Body of Christ.

Dr. Cecilia Jackson

www.ingramcontent.com/pod-product-compliance
Lightning Source LLC
LaVergne TN
LVHW051710080426
835511LV00017B/2840